MINECRAFT ULTIMATE BOOK OF TRAPS

Unbelievable Secrets and Ideas on how to Create and Avoid Traps You Couldn't Imagine Before!

Minecraft
Library

Table of Contents

Introduction

Minecraft is a game about creating and using your imagination. But did you know that fighting other players is a great way to play?! Player versus Player, or PvP, Minecraft servers are very popular and are very fun. If you want to play PvP, but are terrible with a sword, you can use Traps to defeat your enemies!

Great Examples

This chapter of the book will show you great builds that can be enhanced by the use of traps! These builds can use traps as defense mechanisms, to keep out mobs and greifers!

Castle

Traps can improve and protect the integrity of any design, but castles seem to be the perfect place to add traps! From trap doors to lava chambers, a castle can be a nightmare to a potential victim!

Mansions

Like castles, mansions are a very suitable place for traps. Protect your lavish design from griefers and creepers by installing multiple trapping systems!

Railways

If railways are often a vital component of your builds, protect them by installing traps! Activator rails and TNT carts work perfectly in a railway environment.

Caves

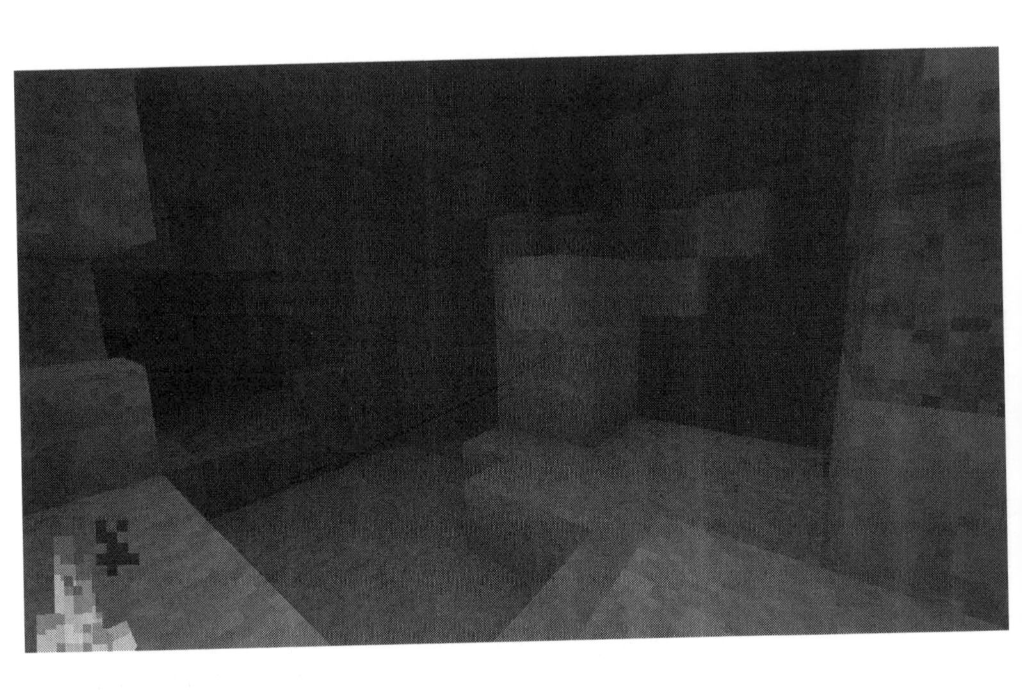

Another great place to hide traps is in caves. Unsuspecting victims won't even know what hit them!

Underground Cities

Protect your hidden metropolis from greifers and mobs by installing a few traps inside the entrance to your beautiful city!

Storage Rooms

When it comes to griefers, storage rooms are always a popular target. Protect your valuables by setting up some protective traps!

Nether Fortress

Nether Fortresses are great places to set up traps, because they are very high-traffic areas, and it is important to protect your Blaze Farm!

Base

While they may be well hidden, Bases are still vulnerable to unwanted guests! Set up a few simple traps to stay safe.

Basics of Trapping

Traps can be very complex machines to extremely simple and basic devices. However, no matter the complexity of the trap, there are always 3 major components; The Trigger, which will activate the trap, The Mechanism, which is connected and activated by the trigger, and finally The Method, which is how the trap works as a whole.

Trigger

The trigger component of a trap is what starts everything off. It can be activated by an unsuspecting enemy, or by the mastermind who created the trap. Buttons, Levers, Redstone Torches, pressure plates and daylight sensors are all commonly used triggers.

Depending on the trap, Triggers can be made extremely obvious or very well hidden. A Trigger could be disguised as a simple door-opener, or it could be placed under 5 blocks of water. An important point to make, however, is that your victim cannot realize that a trigger is actually a trigger, or your whole trap might be at risk.

Mechanism

The mechanism of a trap is the device that is activated, by the trigger, to start the chain of events that will lead to the trap's success. Mechanisms are usually redstone circuits hooked up to a device, such as a piston or dispenser.

Mechanisms can range from large redstone contraptions to a simple redstone torch. Redstone timers are a common mechanism to be used in traps.

Method

The final component of a trap is the method. This refers to how the victim is actually killed. Many different things can be used as the Method in a trap, but some of the most common include water, lava, mobs, falling and suffocation.

Water can be used as the Method of a trap, as it can cause victims to drown. Lava is also a very common method, although it causes any loot to be destroyed. Hostile Mobs can be used as the Method by killing your victim for you. Fall damage is one of the most common methods, as it is simple and you can obtain all the victim's loot. Finally, suffocation can be used as a method, by causing sand or gravel to fall on your victim's head.

Fundamental Concepts

In order to be a successful trapper, you must know and understand the basics. Fundamental Concepts will help you learn and give you insight on how to become the best trapper possible.

Trust

This is a very simple concept, yet it is one of the most important to master in order to be successful. Creating a false sense of trust with your victim opens up many more opportunities to turn around and throw them in one of your traps! You should try your best to gain your victim's trust.

Surprise

It should come at no "surprise" that, in fact, surprise is one of the fundamental concepts in trapping! This concept is pretty simple, but very hard to use. It is important to try your best to surprise your victims into one of your traps!

Greed

This concept is something that you will not be able to control, but you can try your best to promote. As harsh as it sounds, it is natural to be "greedy" in Minecraft! Exploit this trait in your victims by setting up traps that involve them taking precious items.

Obviousness

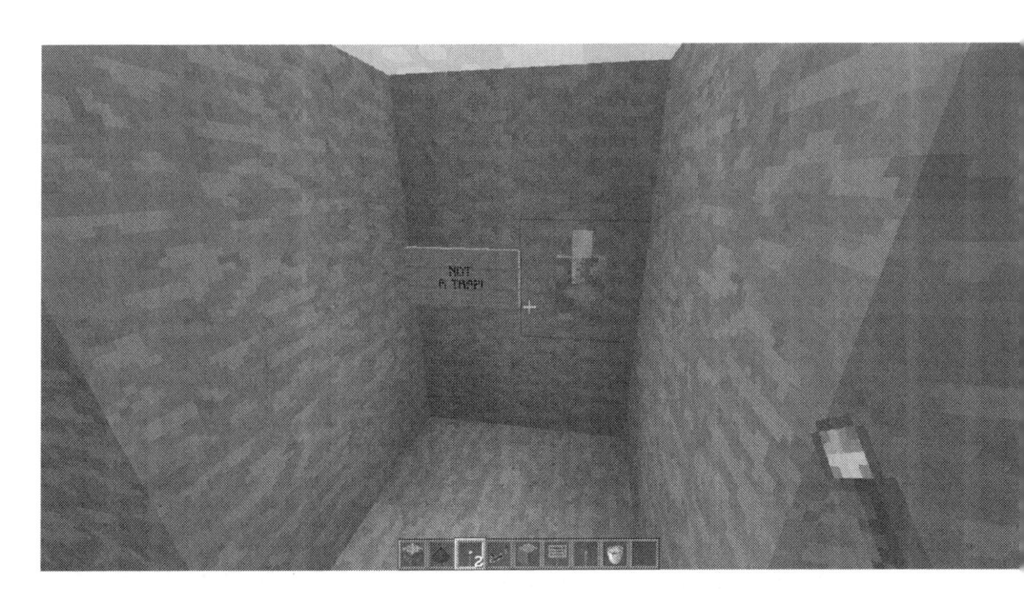

This concept uses the “reverse phycology” theory to trick your victims. Create a trap that looks obvious, so your enemies will turn away from it and run into a much less noticeable trap!

Curiosity

Minecraft is a game about imagination, and thus requires one to be somewhat curious. This concept is to place a trigger that will make the victim curious of what it does. For example, placing a lever that has a "Do not Touch" sign above it will make it likely that somebody will pull it!

Trapping Ideas

This section will give you ideas about different types of traps. There are many different styles and designs of traps to be made, but this guide will show you some of the best!

TNT Based Traps

This chapter is all about traps that use TNT to destroy the victim. TNT based traps are usually simple and effective, but can cause lots of damage! Be cautious where you put TNT traps, as they could destroy your builds instead of protect them!

TNT Mine

A TNT Mine is one of the simplest and easiest traps to build. All that is needed is TNT, pressure plate, and a solid block.

To create this trap, you must first find a spot where your victims frequently travel. Find a block that they are very likely to step on, then dig 2 blocks down. Place 1 TNT block in this newly created hole, then place a solid block on top. This block should be identical to the ones around it. Place a pressure plate on top of the solid block.

The trigger for this trap is the pressure plate. It will be activated when the victim steps on it. The mechanism is simply the TNT block, which will be activated by the pressure plate. Finally, the method of this trap is TNT explosion, which will likely kill your enemy.

The downside of this trap is the obvious "hiss" created by activated TNT. Victims may be able to move out of the way before the explosion. However, the simplicity of this trap make it a favorable option for those with little resources.

TNT Mine Trap – Sophisticated

This is a more advanced and complicated version of the TNT Mine trap. It involves multiple pieces of TNT, and a large area, with a floor made out of stone or oak planks, preferably.

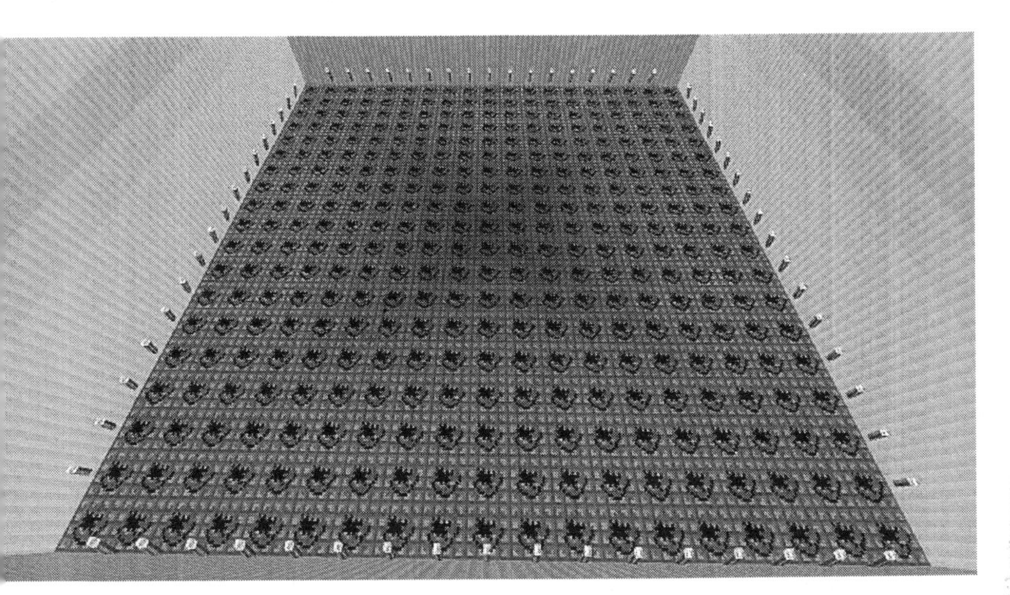

This trap is created by placing several pieces of TNT under a stone or oak plank floor, then placing the respective pressure plate on top. Stone and Oak Planks are the best material to use for the floor, as it will hide the pressure plates from obvious view.

The trigger, mechanism and method of this trap are all the same from the basic TNT Mine trap. When a victim enters this TNT filled room, they will unknowingly step on one of the hidden pressure plates, blowing them up.

This trap still has the downside of the obvious "hissing" sound from the TNT, however it will be more difficult for the victim to escape, as the room will be filled with more mines.

Double Lever Rail Trap

This trap involves using railways. It is the perfect trap if you have a base that is accessed by a railway. For this trap, you will need a TNT minecart, powered rails, redstone dust, redstone torch, solid block, and a regular minecart.

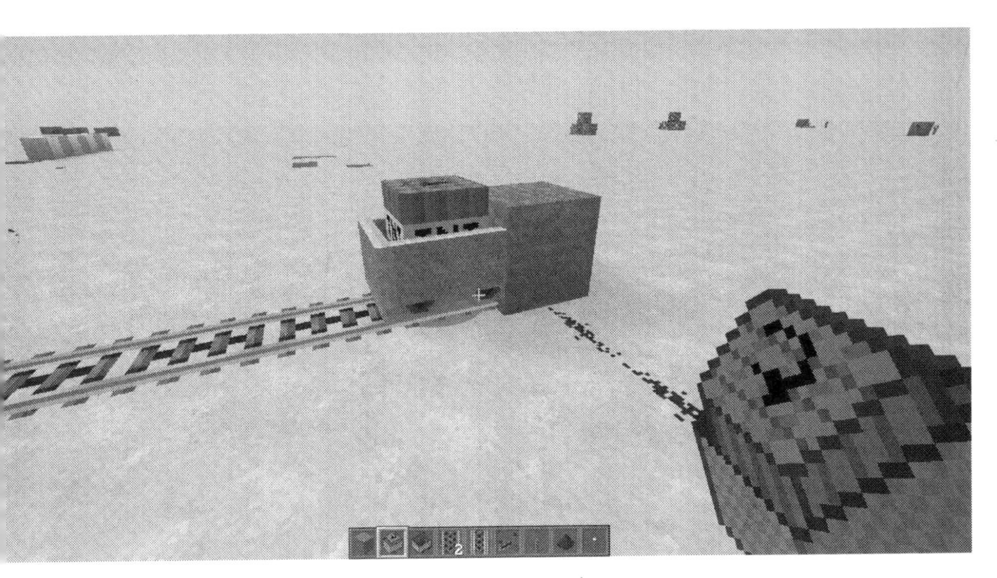

To create this trap, you will need to run a ine of redstone off your last powered rail on your original railway. This redstone should lead o a second railway, which will have a TNT ninecart at the starting position. This second ailway should also lead to a junction point with he original. Now, when somebody uses the original rail, the TNT minecart will be activated, which will cause it to move forward into the original rail.

For this trap, a minecart is used as the trigger. When somebody uses the minecart, the trap will be activated! The mechanism of this trap includes the redstone current and the powered rails, which will be activated by the minecart, as well as the TNT. The method of this trap is explosion, just like all other TNT based traps.

While this trap is very effective, it does have
ome negatives. First of all, the TNT will blow
p the original rail, which will need to be
epaired if you plan on re-using it. Secondly,
his trap may be activated if you are using the
ail. We have created a simple solution to this
roblem, which involves using a piston and a
ever. This design will be demonstrated in the
ext segment.

TNT Rail Trap – Authorized Use

To create and automatic "off switch" for this trap, break one piece of redstone dust, and dig one block down. Replace the dust on the lower block, and it will still connect to the others. Next, you will need to add a piston 1 block back from this. Place any block you want in front of the piston, and one block beside it. On the block beside, place a lever. Now, if you want to use the rail without activating the TNT, just hit the lever!

Swimming Pool Trap

This design demonstrates another way the basic TNT mine trap can be used. This trap requires TNT, pressure plates, sand, and water.

To build this trap, dig out an area where somebody would likely pass. This area should be in the desert biome. Dig 4 blocks down, then fill in with TNT. Place sand on top of the TNT, then pressure plates above that. Now, fill the area in with water. It should look like a natural pond! When somebody jumps in, they will activate the TNT and blow up!

This trap improves on the basic TNT mine trap for a few reasons. First, it prevents the victim from escaping the TNT blast, as water drastically slows down movement. Secondly, the water used in this trap will mask out some of the “hiss” sound caused by TNT. Finally, this trap is an improvement because the water will lower the damage radius and cleanup time.

Greedy miner TNT trap

This is a great trap for a Survival PvP server! Victims will be drawn right into the trap, so you don't even need to do any work!

This trap requires TNT, Daylight Sensor, Redstone, and a rare block. This trap is activated when somebody breaks the rare block, such as diamond ore, and exposes the Daylight Sensor to sunlight! To build this trap, place a daylight sensor, then a piece of redstone beside it, which will run into some TNT. Above the daylight sensor, place your rare block of choice. Cover up the rest of the redstone with anything you like,

The trigger in this trap is the Daylight sensor, which, when activated by sunlight, will power the redstone and TNT mechanism. This trap also uses the explosion method to kill your enemy.

This is a very effective and simple trap, but it have one major flaw; it only works during the daytime. If somebody breaks the block at night, there will be no sunlight to activate the daylight sensor, thus ruining the trap.

Greedy Miner Trap v2

This version of the Greedy Miner trap uses pistons instead of a daylight sensor to activate some TNT. Once a block is broken, specifically a rare block, a piston will retract, which will pull back a piece of TNT onto a redstone block!

To build this trap, you will need a sticky piston, TNT bock, redstone torch and a rare block. To create, all you need to do is place the sticky piston, then a rare block of choice behind it. Beneath the rare block, place a redstone torch. This will cause the piston to push out. Underneath the piston arm, place another redstone torch. Place a TNT block at the end.

This trap uses a solid block as the trigger. When the block is destroyed, it will break the redstone mechanism, which will cause the piston to retract, along with the TNT. When the TNT moves, it will be activated by the redstone torch below!

This trap is very simple, and it works very well. The success rate is high, and there are no downsides! This trap is recommended if you have victims who you know will risk everything to gain another diamond.

Lava Traps

In this chapter, Lava based traps will be discussed. Lava is a great tool for traps because it has a very high success rate, however any potential loot from your victim will be destroyed. Water, on the other hand, in not always as effective as lava, but all the loot from your enemy will be intact. Choose your method wisely.

Lava Trap Room

This trap uses lava to burn up your enemies! For this torture chamber, you will need a door, lever, dispenser and redstone. Of course, lava will be needed as well.

To build this trap, you will need to construct a room with any block of your choice. A good idea is to make ait out of obsidian, then line the walls with stone, so your victims will not be suspicious. Add and iron door anywhere in the room, and place a lever 2 blocks away. Behind this lever, create a redstone wire that leads to a dispenser filled with lava. The dispenser could be places in the ceiling, or a darker area of the room.

This trap uses a simple lever as the trigger. It will be activated when your victim pulls the lever, thinking it will open the iron door. Since iron doors take a long time to break, as well as obsidian, your victim will be stuck to burn! The lever activates the redstone and dispenser mechanism, which causes lava to be the method of death!

While this trap has a high success rate, it doesn't come without issues. The major concern with this trap is that your victim's loot will most likely be destroyed by the lava. Another problem this trap faces is the cleanup; it may be hard to get all the lava out of the room!

Lava Floor Trap

This trap uses carpet to disguise dispensers, which will pour out lava once activated. This is a great trap for a small room, where greifers may come to raid.

For this trap you will need carpet, redstone, dispensers, lava buckets, and a trigger of your choice, preferably a button, pressure plate or lever.

This trap uses whatever trigger you have chosen, which will activate the dispenser mechanism. This trap uses the lava method to burn your victims!

This is a very effective trap because of how well hidden it is. Your victim will not suspect anything until it is too late! Like all lava based traps, the downside is that any loot from the victim will be destroyed.

Lava Wall Trap

This trap uses the same concept as the lava floor design, but instead uses a painting to disguise the dispenser. The benefit of this trap is that it will be much harder for a victim to escape!

This trap requires all the same material as the last design, but instead of carpet, a painting will be used.

This trap, like the floor model, is very effective at eliminating your enemies. It uses any trigger you chose, which will activate a dispenser full of lava to kill your victim!

Lava Trap Door

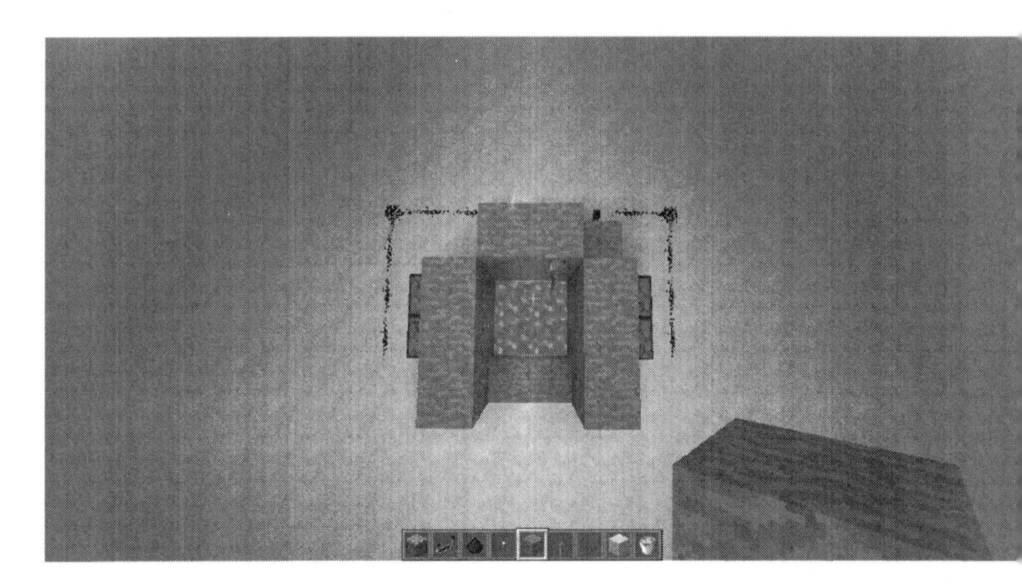

This trap uses sticky pistons and a lava pool to surprise your enemies by dropping them in lava! This is one of the most successful traps, but is somewhat complex to build.

To build this trap, you will need sticky pistons, redstone, redstone repeaters, lava and solid blocks of choice. Any trigger can be used as well, but a lever or button is recommended.

First, dig a 2 x 6 rectangular shape in the ground. In the middle 4 blocks, dig another block down.

Place sticky pistons on the sides of this hole, like shown. Place any block of choice in front of the pistons.

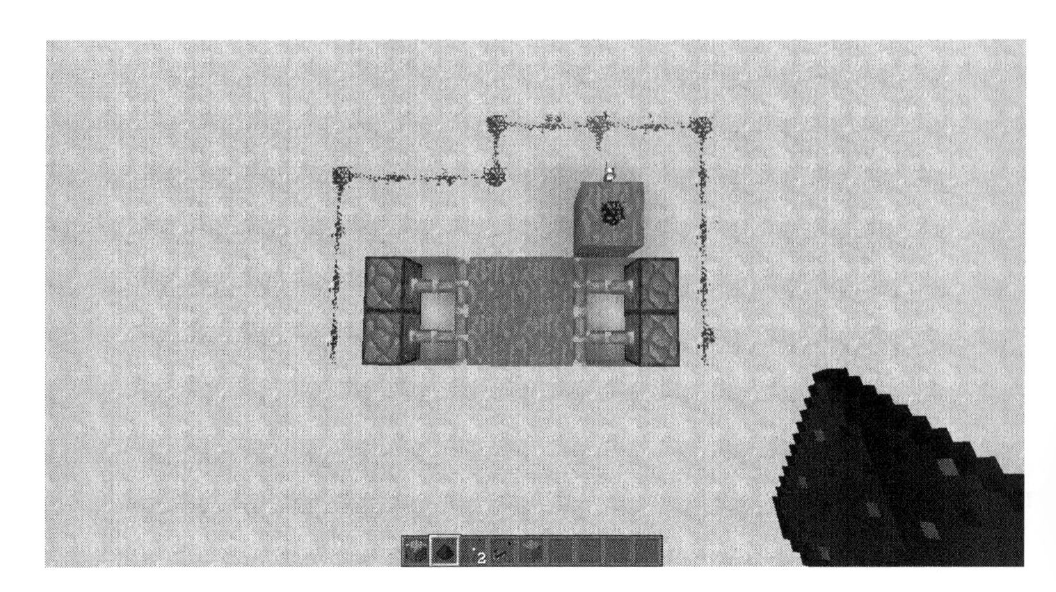

Place redstone dust on the blocks behind the pistons. Wire the redstone to an inverter, like shown. You can do this by placing a piece of redstone, on top of a block that has a redstone torch on it.

Now, construct walls around the 2x2 square. On the wall beside the inverter, place a torch. Activate the torch, and the floor will open. Add lava, and shut off the lever

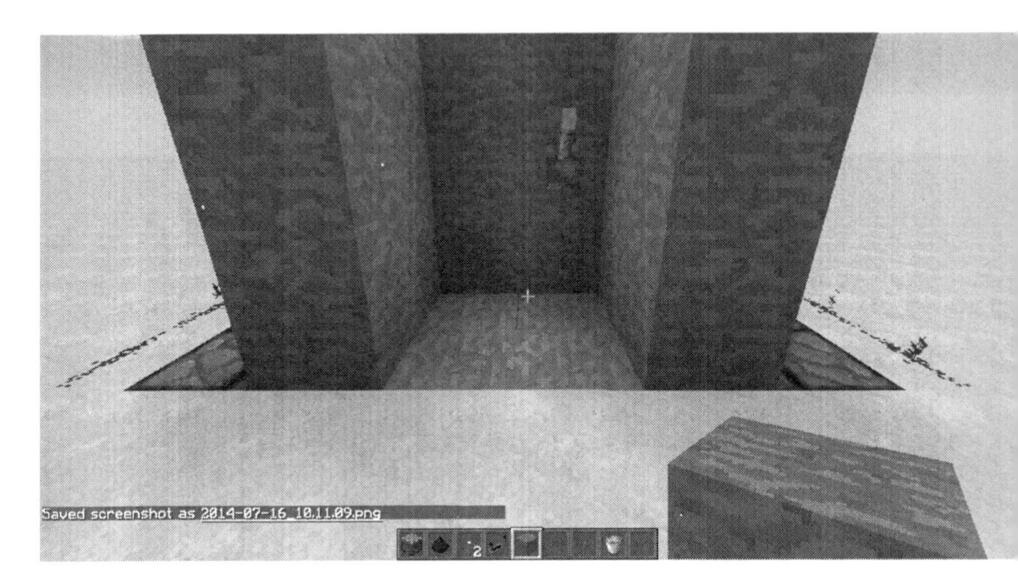

Now, when your victim walks into the room, you can activate the trap, which will cause the pistons to retracting, making the victim fall into the lava!

Conclusion

This guide was designed to teach you all the important ideas and concepts of Minecraft Traps! Please take these lessons and use them to your advantage. You now possess the skills to be a lethal trapper!

Bonus Section

If you liked this **Minecraft: Redstone Ultimate Book**, check out other Amazing Minecraft Books from **Minecraft Library** Creative Creators Community:

1. Minecraft: Ultimate Building Book
2. Minecraft: Ultimate Book of Secrets
3. Minecraft: Ultimate Building Ideas
4. Minecraft: Ultimate Redstone Book

We're delighted to bring you the best knowledge and Minecraft experience. Enjoy!

Minecraft
Library

Made in the USA
Lexington, KY
19 October 2014